S is for Spirit Bear

A British Columbia Alphabet

Written by G. Gregory Roberts and Illustrated by Bob Doucet

Sleeping Bear Press®
310 North Main Street, Suite 300
Chelsea, MI 48118
www.sleepingbearpress.com

THOMSON
★
GALE

© 2006 Thomson Gale, a part of the Thomson Corporation.

Thomson, Star Logo and Sleeping Bear Press are trademarks
and Gale is a registered trademark used herein under license.

Printed and bound in China.

First Printing

10 9 8 7 6 5 4 3 2 1

Library of Congress Cataloging-in-Publication Data

Roberts, Gregory.
S is for spirit bear : a British Columbia alphabet / written by Gregory
Roberts ; illustrated by Bob Doucet.
p. cm.
Summary: "This A to Z pictorial showcases the history, geography, famous
people, and provincial symbols of British Columbia. Topics include, ferry boat,
spirit bear, dogwood flower, and Capilano Bridge. Poetry introduces each topic
followed by detailed expository text"—Provided by publisher.
ISBN 1-58536-291-3
1. British Columbia—Juvenile literature. 2. Alphabet books.
I. Doucet, Bob. II. Title.
F1087.4.R63 2006
971.1—dc22   2006002186

To Erinn,
who loved me before I was anything.

GREG

@

To Susan. And the music.

BOB

A is for Aboriginals,
the First Nations of our lands.
The Ashcroft, Ahousaht, and Alexis Creek
are just a few of the many bands.

It is fitting that the first residents of British Columbia, the aboriginal peoples who lived here for thousands of years before the European settlers came to the area about 200 years ago, are the first topic of this book. In 1778 two ships were discovered floundering in the fog off the coast of Vancouver Island and escorted to the safety of Yuquot (Nootka Sound) by First Nation guides. The captain of the ships, James Cook, and Chief Maquinna made the first contact between the British and aboriginal people in this area.

At that time almost half of all the First Nations People in Canada lived in British Columbia, and their language and culture were some of the most sophisticated in the world. Although the population rapidly declined due to infection from new diseases brought over by the Europeans, there are currently about 200 distinct aboriginal bands in our province, the most in Canada. The First Nations are a significant part of life in British Columbia, contributing immensely to the art forms, identity, and communities.

Of the 16 different species of bats found in British Columbia, eight are found nowhere else in Canada. The Okanagan Valley is the best place to see the furry, nocturnal creatures because 14 types of bats make the warm valley their home. The largest British Columbia species—the big brown bat—lives on Vancouver Island and has been known to sneak inside the legislative buildings and zip above the heads of our provincial politicians.

Bats are the only mammals that can fly. Some bats beat their wings 20 times per second and reach speeds of almost 40 kilometres per hour! They can navigate and catch insects in total darkness because of a special "sight" called echolocation. The bat emits a high-frequency sound wave that hits an object and then is reflected back like light from a mirror. A bat then uses its large ears, and nose, to catch and process the "echo picture" and thereby determine the position, distance, and shape of objects.

Bb

B is for BC Bats,
who see through "echolocation."
With 16 species native to BC,
we're the Bat Capital of the nation.

C is for the Capilano Bridge,
two cables anchored tight.
More squeamish visitors turn around
when they see its daunting height.

C
c

Of all the attractions in British Columbia, this footbridge found in North Vancouver is the most popular. Each year over 850,000 brave visitors cross the 137 metre long and 70 metre high suspension bridge. In 1889 George Grant Mackay, a Scottish civil engineer, purchased a chunk of land that was separated by a huge ravine containing the Capilano River. In order to cross from one part of his land to the other, he built the world's longest suspension bridge out of hemp rope and cedar planks. The First Nations people called it the "Laughing Bridge" because of the noises it made as it swayed in the canyon wind. Although the bridge still creaks and sways, the newest version, made of thick wire cables with 13-tonne concrete encasings at each end, is plenty strong. In fact, you could drive 20 of Victoria's double-decker buses onto the bridge and it still wouldn't break!

D d

D is for the Dogwood flower—
on spring branches blossoms float.
Once, dogwood flowers were sold as pins,
to buy soldiers winter coats.

In 1956 British Columbia officially adopted the Pacific dogwood as its floral emblem, but its significance to the province was established much before then. During the hard times of World War II—when supplies were low—the sale of dogwood lapel pins provided money to purchase wool and other needed comforts for British Columbian soldiers.

The hard, straight wood of the dogwood tree has many historical uses including bows, arrows, knitting needles, and piano keys. The original name, "dagwood," came from its use in constructing "dags" (short for daggers or skewers) and over time became dogwood. The striking white or pink flowers bloom in the spring, and in the autumn the branches flaunt bright clusters of red berries.

Born in Victoria, British Columbia in 1871, Emily Carr, one of Canada's most beloved artists, started her career by drawing a picture of her family's dog on a paper bag with a charred stick. At eight years old, she had found her two greatest joys—painting and animals.

Later in her life Emily produced her famous landscape works by capturing the dynamic, haunting beauty of the Canadian west coast through her wavy, expressionist style. Emily gained much of her artistic inspiration from residing with First Nations people in Ucluelet. They nicknamed the jovial visitor "Klee Wyck," which means "laughing one."

Emily loved animals, and shared her studio with many cats, birds, rats, dogs, and, most famously, her monkey named Woo. Woo was always well dressed because Emily would sew delightful dresses for Woo to wear around Victoria. Emily also funneled her creative energy into writing. Her first book, *Klee Wyck*, won the Governor General's Literary Award, and *The Book of Small* was named the Canadian Book of the Year.

E e

E is for Emily Carr,
with her artist soul and artist hand.
She inspired us with her written word,
and her paintings of our land.

F f

F is for the Ferryboat Fleet
with its familiar sound to warn.
Connecting our land over icy blue
and blowing its deep foghorn.

The British Columbia ferry system is one of the largest and most sophisticated in the world. Each year the fleet of 35 ships transports 22 million passengers— a number well over half the population of Canada (about 33 million). They have even delivered 21 babies on board! The newest ferries are 168 metres long (about the length of two football fields), can carry 470 cars, and sail between the two parts of our province that were separate colonies until 1866—Vancouver Island and the mainland. One of the most interesting voyages occurred when 20 crates of live chickens broke loose on the car deck and hundreds of confused fowl ran, flapped, and clucked in all directions, causing a mammoth brouhaha. The ship's crew worked for hours coaxing the chickens from off the tops of cars, down the stairs, and out of the engine room.

The ship's earsplitting horn or "whistle" is a very important signalling device for safe ocean travel. For example, when you hear one long blast, the ferry is about to depart from the terminal.

G is for the Gold Rush.
It was how the province began.
The miners filled BC with business,
and searched for glitter in the pan.

Gg

Thousands of men came to British Columbia in search of fortunes made of the soft, elusive, yellow rock called gold. A few hit "pay dirt" (literally, ground with gold, or money, in it). Many more didn't. First they rushed to the Charlottes, then up the Fraser River, and into the Cariboo, leaving a trail of roads, businesses, and cities in their wake. Victoria was the stopping point for many miners who had given up on the California rush and had big hopes to strike it rich in British Columbia. In three months during the summer of 1858, the village of just 800 people received about 30,000 miners—roughly 350 a day! Many had to live in tents on the streets while they prepared for their trek across the Strait of Georgia to the mainland. Some, who survived the perilous journey all the way to Cariboo, were handsomely rewarded. One miner reported that he scooped $150 dollars worth of gold from one pan of river mud!

H is for Harrison Hot Springs,
a town where the Sasquatch has been spied.
The sand sculpture competition is Canada's best,
and is known the whole world wide.

Harrison Hot Springs is a village formed around one of British Columbia's 95 identified hot springs. Hot springs form when water seeps deep towards the Earth's core, is heated, and then rises back to the surface.

The village is also rich in Sasquatch lore. Sightings of the big-footed man-beast in the area are numerous, including a sworn court statement by a man claiming to have been held captive by a Sasquatch family for several days. Additionally, several plaster footprints have been obtained that continue to be of interest to some zoologists. In 1957, the village council launched a public expedition in search of the Sasquatch, but the creature remained elusive.

Harrison is probably most famous for The World Championships of Sand Sculpture, which is attracts master sculptors from all over the world. To date, three Guinness' World Records for the world's highest sandcastle have been set there.

H h

I i

In August 1999 a group of teachers from the Nelson, British Columbia area noticed a lone piece of wood sticking out of a glacier in Tatshenshini-Alsek Park. On closer inspection the wood was a tool that belonged to an ancient hunter. The First Nations people of the area named the young male Kwaday Dän Sinchi, meaning "long ago person found." Scientists determined that the man died around 550 years ago—before Columbus discovered the new world—making it the oldest preserved human remains ever discovered in North America. Amazingly, the glacier preserved his animal-skin robe, woven hat, spear, and leather pouch that contained edible plants and dried fish. Because of the excellent condition of the findings, scientists can determine things about his lifestyle, diet, and even who his relatives are.

I is for Canada's Iceman,
a person found from long ago.
In 500 years he barely aged—
while preserved in ice and snow.

Jade has been used for thousands of years by aboriginal peoples for tools and weapons, and was designated the official provincial stone in 1967. About 100 tonnes of nephrite (a softer variety of jade used in sculptures) are produced in British Columbia annually, supplying most of the world's market. The largest jade Buddha in the world was made from a 13-tonne sample of British Columbian jade and sits in a Bangkok monastery.

The Steller's Jay is most well known for its gruff, raspy call and its shimmering blue body and charcoal coloured head. It can be seen in the coniferous forests of British Columbia and eats acorns, seeds, berries, insects, eggs, and other nestling birds. Females usually have a clutch of four bluish-green eggs with dark brown markings. The Steller's Jay was adopted as the provincial bird in 1987.

J j

Two symbols of our province
will stand for letter J.
Our mineral and official bird
are Jade and the Steller's Jay.

K is for Killer Whales,
the hunters of the sea.
Orcas travel in groups, or pods,
and communicate like you and me.

Being home to over 600 killer whales, the waters of British Columbia host one of the densest populations of orcas in the ocean. Of the three distinct populations, the "residents" are most often spotted by whale watchers and mainly eat salmon. Because orcas are mammals, they often come to the surface to breathe, putting on spectacular displays when they jump out of the water, or "breech."

The "transients" travel in smaller pods of two to five individual whales. They are known for their coordinated wolf-like hunting techniques and have huge appetites. When scientists looked into the stomach of one dead orca, they found 15 adult seals and 13 dolphins!

Orcas communicate with high pitched screeching sounds (sometimes as loud as a jet engine) and use clicks in echolocation similar to bats. Just as we can tell when someone speaks if they are from England or Canada, scientists can distinguish between different pods because most have a unique "accent" or dialect.

L is for the Lumberjacks,
who log-roll in the sun.
Each time that he must chop a tree,
he plants another one.

Forestry was the first industry created in British Columbia and is currently the largest. Logging in our province accounts for about 50 percent of the entire Canadian forest industry. People use hundreds of trees every day for fire wood, to make paper, and to build buildings. It is estimated that, on average, each person on the planet uses a soccer-ball-size amount of wood every day. That is why replanting is so important. Under law, logging companies must replant all areas where they harvest, and maintain these plantations until the trees can survive on their own.

Many British Columbia lumberjacks and lumberjills continue to practice traditional logging skills by participating in "Forestry Sports." Two exciting events are "Birling," and the "Springboard Chop." In birling, also known as logrolling, competitors stand on a floating log and try to make their opponent fall in the water by spinning the log. In the "Springboard Chop" the competitor chops a notch in the tree, inserts a plank into the notch, then chops through the tree while standing on the plank.

Ll

M is for the Mountains,
with snow-capped peaks framed in blue.
As Canada's most mountainous province,
they are almost always within view.

One of the first things most people picture when thinking of British Columbia is vast jagged mountains covered in snow and acres of trees . . . and rightfully so. The eight mountain ranges of British Columbia, including their associated valleys and plateaus, cover about 75 percent of the whole province. The Rocky Mountains are the largest range in North America and run almost the entire length of BC. Mount Fairweather is the highest peak in the province at 4,663 metres.

British Columbia is also one of the most geographically diverse areas on the planet. Besides the mountains, ocean, rivers, and lakes, one can find deserts in the Okanagan Valley, ice fields in the coastal mountains, and temperate rain forests on the northern coast.

M is also for "motto." In Latin, British Columbia's motto reads *splendor sine occasu*, which means splendour without diminishment.

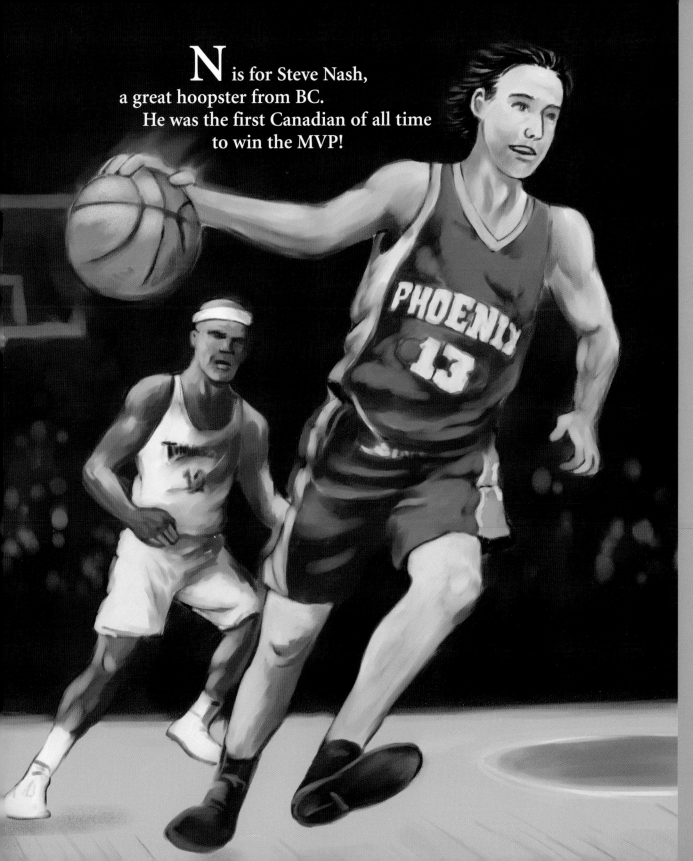

N is for Steve Nash,
a great hoopster from BC.
He was the first Canadian of all time
to win the MVP!

After being named the province's Most Valuable Player in high school, the undersized Nash, who grew up in Victoria, received only one scholarship offer. He took it, and became the University of Santa Clara's (California) all-time leader in assists while helping them to three NCAA tournament appearances. He was then drafted to the NBA higher than any Canadian ever (15th). In 2002 he became the first Canadian named to the NBA All-Star team, then, in 2005, thanks to his amazing team play and league leading assist numbers, Steve became the first Canadian, and only the second non-American to win the league's Most Valuable Player Award. Amazingly, Nash improved his stats in 2006 and became only the ninth player in history to win back-to-back MVPs.

Steve is also one of the league leaders in off-court assists. The Steve Nash Foundation aids thousands of underprivileged children each year in Canada and abroad, by providing access to athletic centers, education, and healthcare.

N
n

O is for the Ogopogo
from the Okanagan Lake.
Although the monster's rarely seen,
only few think he's a fake.

The huge serpent-like creature is widely believed to live in the Okanagan Lake near Kelowna British Columbia, though this has not been proven. Eyewitnesses claim it is 10 to 25 metres long with a head shaped like a sheep's. The first documentation of the Ogopogo is seen in ancient rock art from First Nations people depicting the "N'xa'xa'etkw" or demon of the lake. When canoers were forced to cross over its lair, they would drop a small pig in the water to distract the monster.

The word "Ogopogo" is a palindrome—a word spelled the same forward and backward (try it!). Even though Ogopogo has never been proven to exist (much like the Loch Ness monster), "sightings" continue to occur with regularity. No one has definitively declared that the Ogopogo exists or does not exist, so just to be on the safe side the provincial government has declared Ogopogo a protected species.

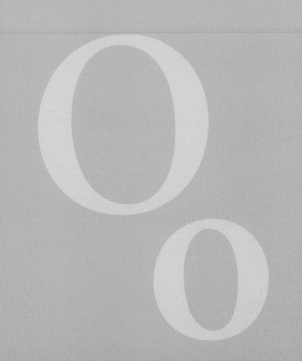

O o

P p

P is for the Pacific Octopus,
which in northern waters can be found.
Their giant arms can spread 10 metres,
and they can weigh 600 pounds!

The Giant Pacific Octopus is one of the most interesting creatures in British Columbia waters. The largest one ever found weighed more than three full-grown men (270 kg/600 lbs), but most weigh around 40 kg (88 lbs), or about the weight of a 10-year-old boy. Each of the eight arms of the Pacific Octopus has hundreds of suckers which are used for touching, smelling, and tasting. They catch their food by pouncing on their prey and then injecting paralyzing saliva. When in danger, a Pacific Octopus can confuse the predator by squirting ink in the water, or by changing the color of its skin to blend in with the environment. The Pacific Octopus is one of the most intelligent creatures in the sea. It can learn to open a jar quickly to get food inside. Other octopi will then copy the behaviour and open other jars after only watching it done once! They also recognise the humans who work with them, and have been observed playing with toys in aquariums.

Q

Q is for the Queen Charlotte Islands,
an archipelago full of unique species.
In the island soil grew the "Golden Spruce,"
the rarest of all trees.

The Queen Charlotte Islands are a large group of mist-covered islands, called an archipelago, found on the northwestern coast of the province. It is the homeland of the Haida nation and is also known as Haida Gwaii, meaning "Island of the People." The relatively isolated region has shaped a unique ecosystem made up of many plants and animals found only here. Consequently, the islands have been nicknamed "The Galapagos of the North."

Haida Gwaii was the site of the only naturally occurring golden Sitka Spruce, "Kiidk'yaas." The 50-metre tall tree that seemed to glow a bright gold amid the dark green branches of its cousins was cut down in a misguided political protest in 1997. When felled, the trunk was as thick as a car. British Columbia mourned the loss of the one-of-a-kind giant, but thankfully, UBC botanists had previously grafted one of Kiidk'yaas' branches, and a mini golden spruce was available to replant in the area.

R is for artist Bill Reid,
and native coastal art's rebirth.
His sculpture *Raven and the First Men*
shows how the Haida came to Earth.

William "Bill" Reid was raised in Victoria and northern British Columbia by his mother, a Haida schoolteacher, and his father, a Scottish-German American. At an early age Bill showed an aptitude for sculpture. While bored at school he often carved a variety of shapes into blackboard chalk, including what would become one of his most prominent themes—the totem pole. After school Bill followed a different path and became a radio announcer, eventually for the Canadian Broadcasting Company. It wasn't until Bill was almost 40 that he left the radio to become a full-time artist. Inspired by a new connection to his Haida heritage, Bill studied the fading artistic tradition of the northwest coast aboriginal people, and through his art and activism, inspired a widespread revival of the craft. Among his many awards, Bill held honorary doctoral degrees from six universities and received both the Order of British Columbia and the Order of Canada. Some of his most famous works, including *Raven and the First Men* and *Spirit of Haida Gwaii* are found on the back of the Canadian 20 dollar bill.

R r

During the months of November through December thousands of Pacific Salmon pack themselves, fins to gills, in British Columbia freshwater rivers like Adams River and Gold Stream. The spawning salmon have just completed an incredible journey starting from the wide-open Pacific. They swim thousands of kilometres upstream, through strong currents and waterfalls, until they find the place they were hatched, sometimes within 60 centimetres! Some scientists claim this phenomenon occurs because the brain of the salmon is sensitive to the Earth's magnetic field (like a compass) and can detect the magnetic field of their birthplace. Others say they can smell their way back. Unfortunately for the salmon, spawning is usually the last thing they do before they die. This produces hundreds of rotting salmon carcasses on the banks of the river as well as a major stench. However, this is a good thing for the ecosystem. The dead salmon seep nutrients into the soil for plants and provide food for other animals like eagles, bears, and otters.

S s

S is for the Salmon
   of Supernatural BC.
If you come during spawning season,
    you'll be surprised by what you see.

T t

Totem poles, carved from western red cedar, are a vital part of the culture of British Columbia First Nations groups. The carvings on a totem display a people's origin, their supernatural experiences, and their achievements. They also show respect to important animal spirits, such as the Thunderbird. The world's tallest totem pole is 52 metres (173 feet) and found in Alert, British Columbia.

The Thunderbird, a huge hawk-like creature, is the most powerful of all spirits. Legend says that the bird would swoop down and snatch whales from the ocean in its huge talons, then return to the mountains to feast on them. Its name comes from its ability to create both thunder, with just a beat of its mighty wings, and lightning, from a blink of its eye.

Tourism is a major part of the provincial economy. In 2003 it contributed roughly $9 billion dollars into the economy. Travel magazines consistently rank Vancouver among the top 10 cities in the world, which attracts many visitors.

T is for the Totem,
an important tourist stop.
The Kwakiutl carved many totems
with a Thunderbird on top.

U is for the Ursus kermodei —
BC's Kermode or "Spirit Bear."
He's not polar or albino,
he's a black bear with white hair.

The almost mystical looking, all-white, black bear is one of the most rare and beautiful bears in the world. The Spirit Bear is generally found in a small, 400 square kilometre range in the the Great Bear Rainforest of northern British Columbia, near Princess Royal Island. When a white pelt was investigated in 1905 by the scientist the bear was named for, Francis Kermode, he thought the bear was either an albino (an animal that lacks the gene for pigment, resulting in white colors and pink eyes), or a totally new species. Later, scientists discovered that they are not albino or a separate species, but a type of black bear that has inherited a recessive gene from both its parents. This is why Spirit Bear cubs are often found with all-black mothers. Native legend says that Raven promised that every tenth bear would be born white. This would be a reminder of when the world was pure and white, covered by glaciers.

British Columbia adopted the Spirit Bear as its official provincial mammal in 2006.

U
u

V is for the capital Victoria,
with her gardens of all kinds.
At night, the harbour's quite a sight
when the Parliament Building shines.

In 1871 after much debate, the old capital of British Columbia, New Westminster, was replaced by the current capital, Victoria. The city on the southern tip of Vancouver Island boasts the mildest climate in Canada, and is often called the City of Gardens. Flowers bloom all year round and hang in baskets on lampposts downtown. Buchart Gardens is one of the world's most famous gardens and attracts more than one million visitors each year, helping to make Victoria the vacation capital of Canada. The famous inner harbour contains two of the city's main attractions: the almost 100-year-old Empress Hotel, and the legislative buildings, which are lit up by over 3,000 lights every evening. The city was named for Queen Victoria, and her English influence is still felt. Often referred to as Canada's most British city, glimpses of "Olde Englande" can still be seen in the horse-drawn carriages, fish and chips, cobblestone streets, and double-decker buses.

W is for Whistler,
a wonderful resort.
Here, winter Olympians will compete
for gold medals in their sport.

In the early 1900s, a small fishing cottage was opened in a secluded valley amid the lofty snow-capped peaks of British Columbia's Coastal Mountains. Alta Lake was principally a summer fishing getaway for the next 50 years, until one man brought his big dreams to the big mountains.

Whistler, now one of the top five ski resorts in the world, is often said to have been built on the Olympic dreams of Franz Wilhelmsen. In 1960, Wilhemsen and his colleagues decided that Whistler, with its heavy annual snowfall and moderate temperatures would be a perfect place to host the Olympics. Unfortunately, bids in 1968, 1976, and 1980 were all turned down. Finally, in 2003, the dream was realised when Whistler was selected to co-host the 2010 Winter Olympics with Vancouver. The community that boasts the most usable ski terrain in North America was named after the hoary marmot which is nicknamed "whistler" because of the sound it makes.

The name Terry Fox holds the **X**.
His gift helps cancer victims cope.
Never before has a marathon
filled the world with so much hope.

X

X

At the age of 18, Terry Fox had his right leg amputated due to bone cancer. During his hospital stay, Terry looked at the dismal plight of the many cancer patients and declared "Somewhere the hurting must stop." The Port Coquitlam resident was determined to be a part of finding the cure for cancer. On April 12, 1980, he officially started the "Marathon of Hope" by dipping his artificial leg in the Atlantic Ocean and starting to run an astounding 42 km every day—about the length of a marathon—across Canada. Although each step caused tremendous pain that often led to bleeding, Terry focused on the pain of other cancer sufferers, knowing each step would support cancer research. Near the halfway point the cancer came back, causing a sharp pain in his chest and forcing him off the road. The disease ended his life, but not his dream. Each year hundreds of thousands of people in over 60 countries participate in the Terry Fox Run that by 2005 had raised over $400 million for the fight against cancer.

Y is for Yoho National Park,
the name means 'wonder' and 'awe.'
You can see Canada's second highest waterfall,
or find the print of a grizzly bear paw.

Y y

Perhaps nowhere else in the world is Mother Nature's work more spectacular than in Yoho National Park. Using erosion, she created some dramatic effects including: a natural rock bridge that spans the Kicking Horse River, and Hoodoos made of immense boulders that balance atop tall pillars. The park, filled with stunning lakes and waterfalls scattered throughout towering peaks, was named "Yoho" from a Cree expression meaning "awe and wonder." Emerald Lake is a jewel of the Canadian Rockies thanks to its deep turquoise color, and Takakkaw Falls, at 254 metres, is the second highest waterfall in Canada (Della Falls on Vancouver Island is the tallest).

The park also provides a habitat for many of British Columbia's animals such as elk, deer, cougars, wolves, and moose. About 60 percent of the world's mountain sheep population live in British Columbia and they are the most common large animal in Yoho. Grizzly bears are also seen roaming the park. It is estimated that about half of all Canada's grizzlies live in British Columbia.

The 200-year-old village near Nootka Sound was named after Lt. Ciriaco Cevallos, one of the original gold-seeking explorers from Spain. In the 1930s Zeballos was again a hot spot for gold rushers. The area was bursting with gold and generated over 300,000 ounces, a sum worth almost $100 million at today's prices. Even the streets glittered, until the owners of a local mine scraped the roads and removed the precious metal. Currently the population is only about 200, and most of the economy is based on logging and tourism. Visitors can still try their luck at panning for gold in the nearby river. Just as in the old days, panning consists of carefully swishing a pan full of dirt in the river. Then, by picking out the rocks and carefully dumping the lighter material out, the gold, a much heavier metal, will collect at the bottom of the pan. What's more, whatever you find in Zeballos, you get to keep!

Z is for Zeballos,
a mining town of old.
The streets in this quaint little village
were once actually paved with gold!

A Rocky Mountain Range of Questions

1. Name the only mammal that can fly.

2. Name four items made from the wood of dogwood trees.

3. What famous artist, born in Victoria, British Columbia in 1871, had a pet monkey named Woo?

4. Where would you be if you were helping crew members gather chickens from the engine room and from the tops of cars?

5. If you were visiting Harrison Hot Springs, what elusive creature might you hope to see?

6. Do scientists believe Canada's iceman lived before or after Columbus discovered the New World?

7. What two provincial symbols begin with J?

8. If you were to look into the stomach of an orca, what might he have eaten for lunch?

9. Name the mountain range that runs along the British Columbia border and name its tallest peak.

10. In what year did Steve Nash become the first Canadian to win the NBA's Most Valuable Player Award?

11. Can you spell the name of a serpent-like creature with a head like a sheep believed to live in the Okanagan Lake area?

12. I use my suckers for touching, smelling, and tasting. When in danger, I can confuse my predator by squirting ink or by changing the color of my skin. What am I?

13. How can rotting salmon carcasses on the banks of a river be helpful?

14. What is the spirit Thunderbird believed to create with a beat of his wings and wink of his eye?

15. What color is the Spirit Bear?

1. Bats
2. Bows, arrows, knitting needles, and piano keys
3. Emily Carr
4. On a ferry boat
5. Sasquatch
6. Before
7. Jade and Steller's Jay
8. 15 adult seals and 13 dolphins
9. The Rocky Mountains are the largest range in North America. Mount Fairweather is the highest peak in British Columbia.
10. 2005
11. Ogopogo
12. Giant Pacific Octopus
13. The dead salmon seep nutrients into the soil for plants and provide food for other animals like eagles, bears, and otters.
14. Thunder and lightning
15. White

G. Gregory Roberts

Greg Roberts fell in love with Canada's greatest province after attending both the University of British Columbia and the University of Victoria. He was born and raised in Lethbridge, Alberta and now lives in Victoria with his wife, who is a budding opera singer and doctoral student. His many talents include barbecuing, making up games for his scout troupe, and authoring young adult novels. Greg also spent two years in the Philippines doing humanitarian service. This is his first book with Sleeping Bear Press.

Bob Doucet

Although originally from Boston, Massachusetts, Bob is pleased to make his home on beautiful Bowen Island off the coast of Vancouver, British Columbia. He studied illustration at Rhode Island School of Design, and graphic design at Kansas City Art Institute. Since opening his own illustration studio several years ago, he has worked with publishers in the U.K., U.S., and Canada, and has over 20 children's books in print, in addition to book covers, editorial, and educational pieces, ranging from whimsical topics to more realistic works, such as *Escape from the Ice*; *Shackleton and The Endurance*, and *The Field Mouse and the Dinosaur Named Sue*. When not making pictures, he plays bluegrass, old-timey and folk music on guitar, mandolin, button accordion and ukulele.